Cat and Dog at the Circus

Cat and Dog at the Circus
© 1999 Creative Teaching Press, Inc.
Written by Margaret Allen, Ph.D.
Illustrated by Catherine Leary
Project Director: Luella Connelly
Editor: Joel Kupperstein
Art Director: Tom Cochrane

Published in the United States of America by:
Creative Teaching Press, Inc.
P.O. Box 6017
Cypress, CA 90630-0017

CTP 2922

Cat and Dog rode the city bus to the circus.

They got their tickets and went in the huge big top.
"Which row are we in, Dog?" asked Cat.
"Row 27," said Dog.

3

"Why did you get seats so far up?" asked Cat.
"The ticket man said they are good seats," said Dog.

4

"When will we get to our row?" asked Cat.
"Soon. Just five more rows," said Dog.

5

Oh, no! Cat's seat had a big box of popcorn on it.
"Who put popcorn on my seat?" asked Cat.

6

Cathy and Cindy said,
"Oops, we left it. We'll take it now."

Cat gave the box to Cathy.

Cat asked, "Where did you get that cotton candy, Cindy?"
"From the man in the red and white coat," said Cindy.

8

Cat got cotton candy and gave some to Dog.
The big top got dark. The circus show began.

Cat said, "It's a long way down.
I'm glad I have my scope!"
"What can you see, Cat?" asked Dog.

"A giant clown in a cute little car
down in the center ring."

"What can you see, Dog?" asked Cat.
"A huge bear out of his cage! Grrr!" said Dog.

12

Cat and Dog had fun at the circus.
On the way out, Cat used the scope one more time.

"What's the last thing at the circus
you can see?" asked Dog.

14

"The last thing I can see at the circus is . . . ME!"

BOOK 22: Cat and Dog at the Circus

Focus Skills: question words, soft c and g

Focus-Skill Words		Sight Words	Story Words
what	ca**g**e	began	candy
what's	**c**enter	some	Cathy
when	**C**indy		cotton
where	**c**ircus		popcorn
which	**c**ity		ticket
who	**g**iant		tickets
why	hu**g**e		

Focus-Skill Words contain a new skill or sound introduced in this book.

Sight Words are among the most common words encountered in the English language (appearing in this book for the first time in the series).

Story Words appear for the first time in this book and are included to add flavor and interest to the story. They may or may not be decodable.

Interactive Reading Idea

After your young reader reads *Cat and Dog at the Circus,* ask him or her these questions: *Who went to the city? Why did they go? Where was the circus held? Which row was Cat and Dog's? What snack did Cat and Dog buy? Who put popcorn on Cat's seat? When did Cat and Dog leave the circus? What was the last thing Cat saw at the circus?*